THE SPIRIT OF THE

GARDEN

THE SPIRIT OF THE
GARDEN

TEXT BY SHELAGH MEAGHER · PHOTOGRAPHY BY JOHN DE VISSER

Stoddart

A BOSTON MILLS PRESS BOOK

CANADIAN CATALOGUING IN PUBLICATION DATA

Meagher, Shelagh
The spirit of the garden

Includes bibliographical references.
ISBN 1-55046-108-7

1. Gardens — Canada — Design. I. de Visser, John,
1930-   . II. Title.

SB473.M43 1995   712'.6'0971   C95-930791-5

First published in 1995 by
THE BOSTON MILLS PRESS
132 Main Street
Erin, Ontario
N0B 1T0
Tel 519-833-2407
Fax 519-833-2195

An affiliate of
Stoddart Publishing Co. Limited
34 Lesmill Road
North York, Ontario
M3B 2T6

Design by Gillian Stead
Printed in China by
Book Art Inc. Toronto

CONTENTS

Scent and visual sensation greet those passing through the doorway in a tall stone wall.
It marks the entry to the inner world of this warm, lush and colorful garden, clearly separated from the house and driveway.

ACKNOWLEDGMENTS

This book would not have been possible without the generosity of the owners who let us photograph their gardens. John and I thank them from the bottom of our hearts for letting us into their special places, showing us around, allowing us to snoop freely at all hours, and even feeding us. Many of the gardens are owner-designed; others have been created by professional landscape architects and designers. To maintain owners' privacy, at their request, no credits or references are given throughout the book, but the professionals whose work is shown on these pages include Dorothea Lovat-Dickson, Tom Sparling, and the author. Douglas Chambers's garden at Stoney Ground is also included.

Finding the gardens in the first place was a task we could not have done alone. Thanks are due to the Civic Garden Centre in Toronto, and in particular to Bayla Gross, Caroline Dalgarno and Robin Wilson, who were immensely helpful in telling us about many of the gardens and putting us in touch with the owners.

A striking red bench lures the visitor to sit and contemplate the garden, while scented thyme and lilies add to the enjoyment.
The bench's bright color also provides zest in winter when the garden is covered in a blanket of snow.

I N T R O D U C T I O N

In 1987 I had the good fortune to study garden design while living in England, a country generally acknowledged to abound in remarkable gardens, both historical and contemporary. When I visited many of these gardens, I felt that they were special places, built by their creators to communicate their own personal visions of earthly paradise. These gardens had real power — power to make one reflect, or marvel, to sense their history, or even to laugh.

When I returned to Canada, I felt, by contrast, greatly disappointed with our gardening lot in life. I muttered about the physical hardships we have to suffer, the shortness of the season, the limited variety of hardy plant material, the lack of a sense of history in our gardens. I thought physical limitations were perhaps the reason why Canadian and northern American gardens failed to move me the way their English counterparts had.

Then, slowly, I began to find gardens here that do possess that same kind of power, and I realized there was more to it than just the physical conditions under which one labors. What was it that made some of these places so special, so evocative? When I looked at the gardens more closely, I found that there are definite consistencies in approach and content, regardless of the gardens' age, size, style or nationality. And that's when the concept for this book was born.

First of all, these gardens have a strong sense of personal expression, just as an author's personality emerges in her story or a sculptor's is reflected in his sculpture. The gardens are woven from the recollected images and symbols of their creators' own special places and times. The gardeners gathered their dreams, desires and memories, and created spaces that evoke that collection of experiences for them and speak of it to others. In so doing, their gardens become as stories, rich in personal detail and possessing meaning beyond the purely visual.

Naturalized dame's rocket (Hesperis matronalis) *lines an inviting mown path, catching the sun that filters through the tree canopy. The flowers' pastel color lends interest without overwhelming the simple serenity of this woodland walk.*

The gardens begin with an underlying theme, intrinsic to the site and meant to set the tone for all that follows. Then, enticing paths, steps and bridges induce the visitor to journey through the garden, while incidents, rewards along the way, capture and engage the imagination. Many of the incidents are symbolic, some very personally and others collectively. Classical statues depicting mythological characters glorify an idealized time and place. Plants brought home as souvenirs from expeditions abroad serve as triggers to summon memories of distant places. A secluded scented lovers' bower covered in climbing roses celebrates romantic love.

The resulting gardens are expressive, taking the visitor on a journey, luring one to a change in perspective, altering a mood. They may evoke pathos, serenity or humor, but whatever their message they have the ability to strike a responsive chord. They are more than just a pleasing arrangement of visual elements.

This book describes the means to magic; how to recognize it, foster it and create it, whatever your garden situation. It begins by exploring what is called the spirit, or genius, of the place — the promise of a garden that is inherent in every site through its natural forms, vegetation and the surrounding land or architecture. Ways of thinking about your own special places play a part in setting the underlying theme. We then go on to detail how different kinds of paths, steps and bridges, the transitional elements, contribute to mood and draw the garden visitor in through a sense of anticipation. In the final section, we illustrate and examine storytelling elements — including, of course, the major role of plants — that set the imagination going.

Cut daisies floating in a sundial birdbath create the simplest of water gardens.

Broad plantings of ornamental grasses are appropriate both in scale and horticultural habitat to dramatize this large country acreage.

A tiny jewel of a garden draws the viewer through the gate toward a cherub statue and beyond. The sense of direction is emphasized by the straight path, clipped border hedge, and the large yews flanking the statue in the background.

Some of the gardens are large, some small. They range from downtown postage-stamp lots to extensive country estates. But whatever their size, they all evoke memories, stir emotions, calm the mind and refresh the spirit.

Charles Moore, in his book *The Poetics of Gardens*, cites the advice of the eleventh-century Japanese author of the *Sakuteiki*, advice every bit as relevant today as it was then:

"Begin by considering the lay of the land and water. Study the works of past masters, and recall the places of beauty that you know. Then, on your chosen site, let memory speak and make into your own that which moves you most."

A sense of the past is created by this folly, constructed to look like the ruins of a barn and offering a compelling view of the garden beyond.

A HISTORICAL PERSPECTIVE

The idea that gardens could be more than just an aesthetically pleasing arrangement of plants and other elements is not new. Historically, pleasure gardens of the Western World were highly representational in their approach, reflecting the attitudes and beliefs of their day. Early Persian gardens developed at the time of Christ — and later appropriated by their Islamic conquerers — were visions of a lush and orderly paradise in the midst of a chaotic, hot and dusty world. Their basic pattern remained essentially the same, with some embellishments, for centuries. A walled space was divided into four squares, at the centre of which was a water source that directed flow outward along the cross axes. Shade-giving and fruit-bearing trees and lush flowering plants were organized in rows, while

Flowers of antiquity, roses symbolized romantic love in medieval Europe and still do so today.

songbirds complemented the sound of moving water. The total effect was cool and fertile in contrast to the outside world. In Islamic versions of the Persian garden, the center represented the point at which mortals and God meet, the water channels the four rivers flowing to the four cardinal points. Their gardens therefore were spiritually as well as visually satisfying.

Gardens of medieval Europe were similarly structured as orderly, walled Edens amid a rough reality. Christian symbols gave them meaning. The cloistered garden with a central fountain represented the Virgin Mary, its straight paths the way of a true Christian. Many of the plants were also symbolic: the rose was love, celebrated in the thirteenth-century allegory "Roman de la Rose"; irises were symbols of Christ; the Madonna lily represent-

Walking gardens such as Stourhead in England are reflected in the design of this large property, which takes the visitor past areas of cultivated garden, through the wood beyond, and back again on a lengthy circular tour.

ed purity; and the three-leaved foliage of the strawberry plant depicted the Trinity.

The Italian Renaissance celebrated a different kind of attitude: humankind as the centre of the universe. Among the many exuberant manifestations of this theme in gardens is the Villa d'Este, built between 1550 and 1580. Water again played a central role, but this time in massive fountains and displays of great engineering ingenuity. The Villa's organ fountain, in its day, played the music of its namesake, and the owl fountain screeched accordingly. During the Renaissance, water represented not only fertility and the abundance of nature, but the Muses as well, sources of intellectual life, in keeping with the rediscovery of classical literature at that time. Also referencing antiquity were myriad statues depicting figures mythological and pastoral, such as the many-breasted Diana of Ephesus, positioned at the heart of the organ fountain.

Classical allegories were also a favorite theme of eighteenth-century English gardens. Here, however, gardens lost their formal structure and sought to simulate and perfect the lines of nature, much as Japanese gardens did and still do. The classics were the basis

The influence of different cultures continues to provide a basis for today's gardens.

Borrowing from the classics, a colonnade provides a cool respite from summer's heat. In time, wisteria and roses will cover the top, providing an even more dramatic sense of enclosure as well as the added pleasure of scent.

The serenity of a dappled glade dotted with spring color is a timeless pleasure.
It can be created by judiciously thinning trees and scattering wildflower seeds.

for a gentleman's education in eighteenth-century England, and the nostalgia for antiquity that the classics create was often reinforced by trips to the glorious ruins of the Italian countryside. So the grand gardens built by wealthy families of the time were punctuated with classical temples and stage-set follies (fanciful structures made to look like ancient ruins).

Stourhead is a brilliant example of this type of representational garden, dedicated to pagan deities of river and springs and mythological heroes. Features such as the Temple of Apollo can be viewed as one journeys along a winding path, the view obscured, then suddenly there in full glory as a corner is turned. The layout pulls the visitor along a route full of such

This drystone wall is dotted with plants collected by its owners from all over the world,
providing them with a botanical reminder of places visited and friends made over the years —
stirring memories every time they walk beside it.

surprises, each one positioned to entice strollers through the garden, and each full of symbolic meaning, often reinforced by a literary inscription.

The evocative qualities of historical gardens originated in the social and religous myths and beliefs, that were reflections of the strong collective consciousness of their days. These gardens were also prerogatives of the wealthy, often vast in scale and grand in effect. How do we translate the concepts behind them to our own, often small sites and limited budgets? The contemporary gardens in this book are still a means to

magic, this time with a modern twist; they are reflective of personal symbols rather than those of social convention. Their creators have "let memory speak" to create oases special to them in individual ways. The whitewashed ruins of an old barn become a re-created Greek villa; a plant collector's winding drystone wall is populated with specimens from all over the world, each with a story about its origins; a tiny, sunken city garden with a womblike ambience provides its owner with a soothing retreat from the bustling world outside its gate.

THE SPIRIT OF THE PLACE

Few places are lucky enough to have such inherent strength of spirit as this site.
The owners have wisely used a gentle hand in its development, keeping the undergrowth thinned, and the meadow shorn,
and providing stepping stones downriver to allow access to further delights across the water.

THE SPIRIT OF THE PLACE

The starting ingredient for a garden is the spirit of the place itself. Many ancient cultures believed that places had actual spirits that protected them or shaped their forms. The Japanese believed that landforms indicated the underlying presence of azure dragons, which represented the male principle, and white tigers, which represented the female principle. The most propitious spots for gardens were where the two met.

In Roman times, each place was thought to have its own guardian spirit or genius. The latin phrase *genius loci*, often quoted by eighteenth-century English garden enthusiasts, came to mean that particular character of a place that shapes our impressions of it. Alexander Pope, eighteenth-century English man of letters, exhorted his patron, Lord Burlington,

A woodland's canopy of leaves sets the mood below by providing an interplay of light and shadow, coolness, and the sound of rustling leaves on a breezy day.

and other landowners to "consult the Genius of the Place in all, That tells the waters or to rise, or fall...." While we no longer believe in dragons or guardians, the idea still holds true that a site has an inherent character that should be tapped as the basis for design.

Many garden sites have a strong mood to them, an impression that they make right from the start. They might be bright, cheerful and open; secluded and enclosed; have a breathtaking view or quiet serenity. This is spirit — the potential for a garden that underlies the site, waiting for us to work with it and bring it out. Obviously, some sites have greater promise than others and will inevitably make gardens of greater impact. But even in relatively unprepossessing spaces, something of worth can generally be found.

The spirit of a small urban lot is largely influenced by architecture, in this case formal, classic and detailed.

Understanding the spirit of the place is important because it is by combining the site's intrinsic possibilities with your own dreams and desires that you create a unified whole. By applying your own imagination to the potential of the site, you determine a style, an underlying premise or theme and the basis for a cohesive overall result.

Determining the spirit of the place involves taking an inventory of all the elements that contribute to its character. There are visual features of course — the physical features of the site, the amount of light or shade — as well as the architecture of the house and even the feel of the surrounding land or neighborhood. How a place feels to us also depends on our other senses, and so we need to consider what we hear, smell and feel as well. It is the layering of all these effects that creates a site's total impression.

The bare trunks of a pine forest with its typical lack of undergrowth create a strong sense of the vertical,
particularly when the angle of the sun's rays plays up the contrast of light and shade.

Natural Places and Their Spirits

Before applying the inventory process to garden spaces, it is useful to think first about various forms of natural landscape and their characteristic features. In a woodland, for instance, the visual experience provides a rich beginning. We see an interplay of light and shadow, the weight and texture of tree trunks rising upward, subtle variations in greens, browns and grays occasionally punctuated by red berries. The total woodland effect, however, is more than this. You feel the coolness of the shade, sense the feeling of enclosure

Variations on a theme, these open spaces demonstrate the calming effect of simple lines and broad bands of harmonious colors. The concept can be translated to fit the smaller scale of a garden just as effectively.

from the overhead canopy and the trunks around you, smell the musky forest floor and decaying leaves, and hear the rustling of leaves, birds and small animals.

Open, hilly farmland sites, by contrast, are characterized by gently flowing horizontal curves and planes with broad swaths of colour provided by fields of bright yellow rape-seed, mellow golden oats, or green pastures. There are open vistas, even light, and the warmth of the sun on a fine day. Without trees to restrict it, the wind makes its presence felt more strongly, whether as a welcome gentle breeze or as a bitter, howling gale.

The geography of the Laurentian Shield area creates a totally different impression. Angular lines and hard planes of heaved rock contrast with the dark greens and soft needles of

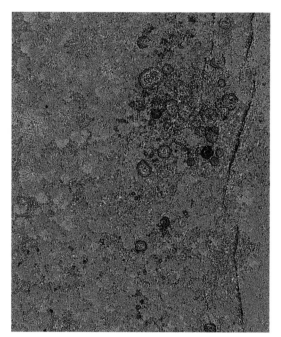

Details such as colorful lichen on a rockface can provide natural artforms and points of interest within a garden.

conifers. Invading lichens and mosses on the rocks bring a sense of detail to the large general scale. Colors tend to the blue side of green and to grays, deep and somber even against a bright blue sky. The scent of pine needles, their quiet crunch underfoot, and the soft sound of the wind in evergreens complete the feeling.

Finally, imagine a narrow river valley with rapids. Here, the rushing water predominates as you hear it tumbling and frothing against rocks, smell its freshness and feel it in the air. It is exhuberant and ever-changing, with sunlight sparkling and jumping off the surface of the moving water. The riverside vegetation and trees are lush and varied, a multiplicity of greens providing a background for the rich colors of blossoms where the sun reaches.

S i t e   A s s e s s m e n t

Now consider your garden site and what character it has, whether it is an untouched natural space or an existing garden that needs remaking.

Space definers. These are the horizontal and vertical shapes that determine the scale and form of the existing space, much as walls, floor and ceiling define a room. The floor, or ground plane, in a garden may be sloped or flat, of smooth grass, rough rock, ground cover or leaf litter. Its basic size and shape determine much of the overall scale and how the garden

The deeply ridged tree bark creates year-round textural interest, while daffodils provide a seasonal spark with their happy, yellow color and promise of spring.

evolves. The walls are created by trees, shrubs, fences and architectural elements such as houses and garages. They help define scale by their size and placement, and the degree of openness or enclosure of a site. Tree canopies or overhead structures such as pergolas and awnings may create ceilings, though there is often no perceived ceiling save the sky.

Light and Shade. The quality of light in a garden influences its character a great deal, and that character can change dramatically with the seasons, the time of day and in different areas of the site. It is best to observe the varying qualities of your garden's light over time to get a true picture of its impact. A site with many deciduous trees, for example, will be uniformly shaded, cool and serene in summer, provide dappled, playful changing sunlight in spring and fall, and show strong, dramatic shadows of bare trunks and branches against white snow in the low, angled sun of winter. A south-facing seating area may be pleasantly sunny and warm at breakfast-time in summer but feel unbearably hot and exposed at midday. One part of the garden may be uninspiring for much of the day, then provide the perfect spot for enjoying a sunset.

Light and shadow are used effectively in this casual garden, where shadows play strongly on the stucco wall and a bench provides a warm or cool retreat, depending on the time of day.

The female aspects of this hillside site are accentuated by curving steps, walls and plantings. Sloping terrain always offers potential for creating a sense of anticipation as visitors work their way through changes of level.

Topography. Hilly sites are intrinsically female, with their curving, fecund forms, while flat sites have an inherent angularity or hardness about them. A slope can be terraced to create a series of level spaces or reshaped to accentuate its curved nature.

Temperature. Temperature is influenced not only by light and shade, but also by exposure to wind and water. The height of a place also affects its temperature, dells being cooler than higher spots. The coolness or warmth we feel is part of our experience of a space and therefore becomes part of our expectations about it. Hence, we see a tree canopy and expect coolness there, or see a place open to the sun and know it will give us warmth. Being in one space and longing for another provides part of the sense of anticipation that leads one through a garden.

Breeze. A gentle breeze can make an enclosed garden particularly soothing in the heat of summer, while a windswept hill has a wild and free feel. As with light, the effects of wind are ever-changing with the day, season and particular area of the garden.

The unmistakable scent of old lilacs wafting through the windows of the house may be reminiscent of grandmother's garden.

Sounds. When you step out the back door, are you greeted by the din of city traffic, the roar of a rushing river, laughing children, the trill of birds, or murmurs of trickling water? Do hear the wind blowing across open fields or filtering through leaves and needles? As with other characteristics of the site, sounds have the capacity to irritate, soothe or uplift. Whether we suppress them or enhance them, they are part of the inventory of features we can work with to create a total effect.

Scents. Our sense of smell affects our impressions of a place in many ways, through association and memory. We all recognize, for instance, a certain scent associated with spring, commonly thought of as the smell of the earth warming up. (It's actually caused by the dying bodies of actinomycetes, the earliest risers of the earth's sleeping micro-organisms in spring.) The scent of lilacs may remind you of your grandmother; pine needles and sap may stir memories of a cottage or a canoeing trip from your youth.

A mature contorted hazel (Corylus avellana) *with its striking form provides a welcome focal point when the thrill of color is over.*

Scent is instrumental to daydreaming and a large part of a garden's pleasures.

Existing features. Especially in an established garden, existing features of a site may strongly influence the spirit of the place. Moss-covered flagstones of an old patio give a sense of history to a garden, as does the dominating form of a craggy, mature tree. An existing fountain may contribute the soothing sounds of gently moving water, and mature shrubs and fruit trees may attract songbirds. Perhaps there is a weathered bench or garden house where generations before

have rested or courted. These all contribute to a spirit of serenity, history and longevity.

Now let us look at some examples of how this inventory process can apply in specific situations, and how situations can be modified to enhance given characteristics.

Consider a house that is nestled in the midst of a treed, five-acre estate lot. The area around the house is fully cleared but the surrounding woods are thick, creating an unsettling contrast between the light, open space and the sudden heavy vertical of the dense trees. What could be a pleasing sense of enclosure might become almost oppressive as a result. To improve this situation, small clearings could be cut into the wooded area and trees thinned at its edge and within its boundaries, to create glades and to blur the division between the two spaces. In this way you create a transition between the lightness around the house and the dark of the woods, with dappled light inbetween. Reducing the density of the surrounding trees makes the forest edge into an inviting space of irregular verticals, rather than an apparently inpenetr-

able wall of trees, yet the sense of enclosure and the interesting contrast between light and dark areas remain.

A home set on the same amount of relatively flat, open land — perhaps part of what was a farmer's field — may appear to have unpromising garden potential. However, in keeping with the feeling of openness that characterizes such a place, one might shape the land into gentle new hills, berms and curves that play with sun and shadows for a subtle re-interpretation of the original site. Add dense groupings of

The undulating form of gently rolling land, mirrored in the line of the fence and pond below,
is accentuated when the angle of the sun plays up the shadows.

evergreens in masses large enough to suit the scale of the place, and the sense of hills and valleys will become stronger and more three-dimensional.

In a suburban, city or town garden, the underlying spirit of the place can be harder to recognize. One way to draw out a distinctive character is to pick up on one key element as a base from which to create a larger impression. A large old tree, for instance, may be your starting point. It has the essence of canopy, shadow and coolness that is a woodland in miniature; this fledgling spirit could be intensified by adding the cooling influence of a water feature, building up a leaf-mulch planting bed around the tree and introducing native woodland plants and mosses there. Placing a bench under the tree's canopy further invites you into this miniature woodland realm.

A larger garden may enjoy a number of areas of

A larger garden may be broken up into a series of rooms. Here the spaces are divided by a dense mass of shrubs, with statuary and a bench drawing the visitor into the area beyond.

different character. A property might have one area of large open lawn, warm from uninterrupted sunlight, smooth with mown grass and in earshot of the street. Turn a corner and you could find an enclosed nook in an L-shaped wall of the house, perhaps on a different level from the lawn, quiet and sheltered but very much a part of the formal structure of the house itself. Farther on, a large tree offers shade and a sense of seclusion. Taking advantage of such differences can give you places within your garden to suit your every mood.

Once you have assessed in this way all of what your garden site offers, it's time to think about how to manipulate these characteristics to create a garden that is special to you personally. You and the site are collaborators in devising a garden that tells a story about both you and the place itself.

The pink pastel shades of massed Dianthus *harmonize perfectly with a soft blue country house and the rustic wattle fence.*

Enhancing Mood: Harmony Versus Contrast

Physical attributes have an emotional side, conveying mood by their very nature. A dark, enclosed space, for instance, may feel either brooding and melancholy, or perhaps safe and womblike. A high, open space can convey a sense of command, or alternately the sense that human presence is insignificant in the context of such vast surroundings. Some sites exude strict formality, while others have the comfortable feel of a favorite slipper.

Having determined the underlying spirit of the site, the challenge is to enhance that spirit. There are two ways to do so — harmony and contrast.

Harmony involves employing complementary elements to emphasize existing ones. To harmonize the wooded site, light pruning of the overhead leaf canopy can increase the play of light and shade; moss, mulch or pea gravel underfoot will further deaden sound; heavier planting of the periphery can emphasize the sense of enclosure.

Contrast is more difficult to implement. It can result in two concepts simply fighting unsuccessfully with each other. For contrast to work, the spiritual side must usually remain dominant while the opposing element acts as an exclamation mark. In a wooded site, for example, contrast may be achieved by the deliberate creation of small open spaces. These sunlit glades, surrounded by the darkness of the forest, can be planted with a carpet of grasses and wildflowers to further emphasize the verticality of the trees and make a lovely hidden spot to lie on a summer's day.

A pathway of white cut stone maintains the planting theme of monochrome formality.

A formal site might be enhanced by clipped hedges and neat plantings, or be contrasted with softening patches of loose, billowing flowers within its tight structure. Adding a bright primary color or a witty modern sculpture is another way to inject levity into a strict, formal plan.

These two tools of enhancement needn't be mutually exclusive; sometimes magic is best achieved by combining them. In the cosmopolitan garden, materials could reflect the site's city feel, with low brick walls as space dividers and hard paving underfoot. Soft plantings within this environment can then appear even more lush by virtue of their textural contrast with the harder elements. Further contrast is achieved by incorporating the sounds of moving water and planting to attract songbirds, heightening the sense of oasis within a visibly urban environment.

Familiar springtime sights, candytuft (Iberis sempervirens) *and basket-of-gold* (Aurinia saxatilis) *create striking seasonal displays.*

Seasonality

Sites may change drastically in the mood they convey during different seasons. Think how your garden feels throughout the year; there is probably one season where the site is at its natural best. In sun and where perennials dominate, summer is probably the most spectacular viewing time. In shade, spring is often the most exciting time, when the flowers of the woodland floor burst into bloom and the emerging leaves overhead are a shimmering, pale green. Autumn may transform an average garden into a colorful extravaganza of ever-changing leaves.

The physical changes of plants throughout the seasons provide the main source of variety in a garden. Visually, of course, the cycle of rebirth and death is continuously played out, the fresh greens of spring giving way to deeper greens and bright colors of summer, then to the rich tans and reds of autumn, and on to the muted tapestries of winter.

Other senses note the changes as well. Spring gardens smell of damp earth, followed by the scent of blossoms and fresh-mown grass of summer, then to the distinctive autumn odor of fallen leaves. The mating

This startling blast of spring color is later replaced by annuals, a maintenance-intensive but effective means of ensuring strong color throughout the growing season.

calls of birds give way to the soft buzzing of bees and the heavy hum of cicadas in summer, changing to the sound of crisp, fallen leaves swirling in the wind.

A single-season garden can have its appeal extended further through the year by carrying some of its best elements into other times of the year. Perennial borders can present a splash in spring when underplanted with masses of bulbs, which will die down as the perennials take over. A shady site can come alive again in autumn if you include some specimens that color well and fall bulbs such as colchicum.

Large gardens offer greater scope for allowing different areas to present their individual, seasonal tours de force with little concern for how they will look the rest of the year; one simply doesn't venture into that area in its off-season. In this kind of garden, every occupant of the midsummer perennial bed, for example, is blooming at the same time. There are no plants that have already performed, and none waiting in the wings. This kind of spectacular, single-season perennial border was made famous by English designers such as Gertrude Jekyll earlier in this century, in gardens where space was not an issue. In most of today's smaller gardens, however, such a focused effort generally results in a drab view the rest of the year.

This formal house is well served by the controlled forms of clipped evergreens and low groundcovers. Various shades of green contrast subtly with the neutral stucco of the facade, while the barest hint of color comes from a smattering of red annual geraniums.

The Influence of Architecture

The smaller the garden, the more the house is going to influence the character of the site. Conventionally, garden areas near a house are more controlled in style, while further away from the building, they are allowed to become more wild and natural. It's as though our sphere of influence radiates from our homes, losing strength along the way.

The degree to which gardens evoke human influence versus nature's landscapes has provoked centuries of debate and changing fashion. In eighteenth-century England, Capability Brown sought to bring the countryside, in idealized form, right to the front door of his clients' palatial homes, eliminating fences, walls and mazes completely.

A study in contrasting textures, clipped yews and springy grasses surround a weathered shingled outbuilding. The bulk of the yews is sufficient to carry the mass of the building visually.

Versailles, on the other hand, where 250 acres of meticulously clipped avenues emanate from the palace's facade along two central axes, extends the formality of Louis XIV's palace out until it seems to merge with the infinite distance. Although both cultures brought down the walls that had enclosed gardens for centuries, the French sought to dominate the surrounding landscape while the English sought to embrace it.

Today, on properties minuscule by comparison, the garden's role as a unifying force between a house and its grounds is no less diminished by the reduced scale. The style of the house generally leads the way. If the objective is visual harmony with the house, then mirroring its materials and style in the surrounding garden will help give the whole a strong sense of coherence. Alternatively, applying the tool of contrast can have dramatic results but is considerably more difficult to do well, as one risks having a house and garden that simply do not relate to each other.

Identical pots of annual geraniums accent the repetitive pattern of a balcony balustrade.

The brick of the house is carried into the garden in a curving wall, uniting house and landscape.
Clipped plantings complement the formal architecture.

A classic entryway is treated with understated polish: a pair of color-coordinated black urns bearing geraniums balance the shock of red in the door.

The technical style of the house's architecture often becomes the dominant character of the site. This is especially true for the front face of a property, where house and garden tend to be viewed together and present the first impression of the property as a whole. A log cabin, for example, is definitely casual and natural. Clipped boxwood hedging would look at odds with such a structure, whereas a wildflower meadow or kitchen garden would feel much more appropriate. Paths would be made of rough, randomly shaped flagstone or gravel, and shrubs would be allowed to grow naturally.

The formality and perfect symmetry of a grand Georgian home, on the other hand, calls for a more formal garden, at least close to the house. Square-cut flagstone or brick paths, clipped shrubs and a subdued color palette echo the style of the architecture. Here, a wildflower meadow would look messy by comparison. In a larger property, the formal parts of the garden closest to such a house can give way to looser, less formal plantings and features in the farther reaches of the garden.

Between these two extremes are many other styles. It is by seeking out their defining characteristics that you will gain clues as to how your garden can best be designed. Look at the architecture's overall scale to see if it is quaint or commanding. Consider its basic form. Does it present a uniform front with a symmetrical layout, which suggests an ordered garden, or does it have asymmetrical nooks and crannies and protuberances? Is it classic, old-fashioned or modern?

Think about your home's details. If it has the ornate gingerbread of a Victorian house, the garden may echo the treatment with fancy wrought-iron railings, trellises and a colorful flower mix, or it may be kept simple, with straight picket fences and shaped shrubs to let the details of the house stand out in contrast. If it is austere and understated in its details, an ornate approach to the garden may spoil its simplicity.

Beyond overall style, there are also the shapes, forms and textures of the house that can be repeated or contrasted in the surrounding garden. A rounded archway over the front door might be reflected in a semicircular cascade of steps leading up to it. Simple, angular lines can be mirrored in the lines of the garden. Stone used as a facade on bay windows can be repeated in the front walkway to tie the architecture to the landscape. The nubbly texture of a stucco house might be contrasted with perfectly smooth limestone on a terrace.

Architecture influences not only through style and detail, but also with respect to the shape and positioning of a house on its site. Note its relationship with the garden — does it enfold the space, perhaps in an L shape or with a courtyard? The garden could be built up around this central, womblike core. Does it meet the garden head-on with a straight expanse of brick and windows? Architectural elements such as patios and pergolas may be necessary to connect the two. A house that

A trellised structure in the garden helps create the sense of separate rooms, as in a house.

sits lower than its garden may allow for a sunken patio area that gives a feeling of intimate enclosure; a house sitting higher may call for a seating area that commands a view of the rest of the property below.

Houses are often positioned so that the back is not neccesarily the optimum place for traditionally back-of-house activities. A sunny front could mean moving the main patio there. One side of the house may provide an opportunity for a small, intimate garden away from both the bustle of the street and the noises of other family members at play.

Consider, too, the perspective of being inside looking out onto a garden. A small space fully enclosed with high fences or plantings can give the impression of being an outdoor room, a seasonal extension to the house. Its potential can be used to advantage by opening up the house to it, replacing walls with glass doors and windows for a continuous flow of space. The style set by the house's interior can then be translated into the garden, blurring the distinction between outside and in.

Providing a link between house and garden, this large porch reflects the scale of both, its columns echoing the mature trees beyond.

Splendid neighboring views such as this one are perfectly accented by the soft springtime yellows of naturalized daffodils massed in the foreground. A flagstone border unobtrusively signifies the end of the manicured lawn area.

The Context of Neighborhood

No site is an island, devoid of visual contact with neighboring properties. The surrounding neighborhood or countryside may further define the spirit of a garden space by giving it context in a greater frame of reference.

In cities, many back gardens are relatively self-contained spaces, but the influence of neighborhood is usually powerfully felt in the front, where visually the site and its surroundings tend most to collide.

In an urban townhouse's front garden, for example, one can create an oasis of nature in the midst of downtown's concrete expanse. But to maintain a sense of context, the garden will also need some elements of cosmopolitan structure within it. A mass of

An urban setting often calls for a cosmopolitan garden style, executed here with formal classicism.

Playing off the natural landscape, large stones scaled to the surroundings form a casual path
to the front door of a cottage, mimicking the outcroppings indigenous to the area.

wildflowers sandwiched between neighbors of flagstone and boxwood will look as though it wandered from its usual place, took a wrong turn and ended up there by mistake. If you save your expressions of individuality for the back, your home will look more as though it did not long to be somewhere else.

For similar reasons, but with a totally different style, in country and cottage properties the spirit of the neighborhood is intrinsic to the spirit of the property. A cottage site can be enhanced by recognizing and working with the wilder nature of a northern Cottage Country landscape, as the overwhelming beauty of such country would be wasted if ignored. If the cottage architecture is appropriately colloquial, the house, its garden and the natural surroundings can enjoy an almost seamless and satisfying unity. This is not the place for sweeps of manicured lawn or squared-off concrete retaining walls. Indigenous rock, pathways of stone, needles or wood chips, and naturalistic plantings do cottage plots much greater justice.

The walls and floor of an abandoned barn have a whitewashed appearance that inspired this garden,
evocative of Greece in the midst of North American pastureland.
The bright primal colors of plantings stuffed into openings in the concrete further play up the theme.

Determining Your Garden's Theme

Now that you have a good idea of the site's potential and underlying characteristics, how do you begin to impose your own desires upon it to pleasing effect? The purpose behind establishing a theme or concept for your garden is to ensure that the end result looks unified, and to help you focus on what really makes a place special for you. Even if you use the services of a professional designer, this input is critical to the design and can only come from you. After all, in the end the garden is supposed to be yours, not the designer's.

A garden's central concept may be representational, as is Stourhead's winding journey through the classics, but it need not necessarily be so grand in scope. You might build your garden to evoke a different time or place, such as the Greek villa recreated within a barn foundation (shown

This collector's garden is filled with fine examples of roses and lupins, a horticultural extravaganza for expert and neophyte alike. The bench at the far end is the remains of an ancient tree that once grew on the property.

opposite), a medieval knot garden, an English cottage garden or a pioneer's garden. Friendship gardens are built around plants given by friends over the years, with each specimen reminding the owner of the person behind the plant.

Alternatively, the central idea may be to convey a mood in the garden. It may be a still, shaded space for quiet contemplation, an exuberant celebration of nature's colors and forms, or a soft, romantic retreat.

Stylistic themes offer other possibilities, especially where the architecture of the site has a strong style on which you might want to expand, such as minimalist Modern, heavily adorned Victorian or formal Georgian.

Whatever you choose as the underlying theme for your garden, make sure it suits the site as well as your personal preferences and desires. Then, when

A formal parterre garden makes a grand gesture for the terrace of a large, traditional home.

you've settled on the theme that's right for both, be ruthless about making everything fit it. Your central theme should act as a kind of test for every plant, statue and idea that strikes your fancy. So when you've established a formal French parterre but then fall in love with a spouting frog sculpture you saw on a gar-den tour, ask yourself: Is this a witty little addition, or is it completely at odds with everything else? Is there some other part of the property where it could be put to better use? By the time you've built and lived with your garden for a few years, you should understand your creation sufficiently to know the answers instinctively.

TRANSITIONAL
ELEMENTS

Gardens set behind tall brick walls with solid doors possess an atmosphere of total privacy from the outside world. The open door beckons with irresistible allure to explore the oasis within.

T R A N S I T I O N S   T O   T H E   I N N E R   W O R L D

In the fairy tales of our youth, every magical place has a gate or key that allows entry to its special world. That idea extends throughout our daily lives, so that how we enter doorways and vestibules sets up our expectations about what's inside, and helps us with the mental transition between places.

Gardens work in the same way. The elements that affect our passage from the outside world to that within the garden strongly influence our reactions to the space, and the degree to which we feel at home in it. The areas of a garden that establish such transitions help people alter their frames of reference and set up expectations of what is to come on the garden journey. Especially at the garden entrance, there must be

Passing through an archway, especially one covered with scented honeysuckle vine, signals all the senses to anticipate a lush experience inside.

ways to help the visitor shed the outer world of traffic, work and worries in favor of the peaceful inner world of the garden, where the pace is slow and day-dreaming is encouraged. Transitional devices may be as simple as a single gate or as complex as a long, winding maze. Whether they take one step or one hundred to traverse, transitions provide the necessary preparation for exploration of the garden within.

As one passes through gates, along paths, over bridges and up steps, a sense of anticipation is fostered and interest is continually refocused on fresh aspects of the garden and its mysteries. With each successive transition, another layer of the outside world is shed and the garden becomes more involving.

Entranceways: Gates and Barriers

An elaborate filigreed iron gate sets the tone for the elegance of the house and garden within.

Gates, and the barriers through which they allow passage, serve the dual purpose of inviting in and shutting out, making them the most obvious symbols of transition. For centuries, people have focused considerable creative energy on devising gates that speak volumes about the gardens and owners within, and the degree of welcome that awaits visitors.

There is a language of entranceways; they communicate through their height and breadth, the simplicity or grandeur of their materials, and the degree to which they allow outsiders to see, or enter, the garden inside.

Tall, impenetrable gates in high, solid fences or walls say "keep out" firmly and imply a closely guarded love of privacy. For those inside such gates, of course, the feeling of escape from the outer world is much stronger, allowing the garden to envelop its visitors more fully. Not only is there a distinct visual boundary, but tall structures also inhibit sound infiltration, increasing the sense of sanctuary within.

The grand, filigreed gilt and wrought-iron gates that served as entranceways to many of Europe's great historical houses set the tone for the formal opulence of the grounds and architecture. Generally set in

A partial wall and decorative lamp mark the entry to an inner courtyard and the house.
The opening is just wide enough to be inviting, just closed enough to feel secluded.

Abundant blossoms spilling over concrete steps and a low picket gate welcome guests to this casual and relaxing garden.

brick or stone walls and hinged to massive piers, the gates allowed a tantalizing glimpse of the grandeur within. They made a clear statement about the station of the owners and the degree of separation they enjoyed from the common crowd.

The shorter the gate and barrier, and the more see-through, the more inviting it is to a visitor. By making the distinction between public and private property less clear, such entries imply a greater welcome from the outside. Simple picket gates, for example, bespeak warmth because of their openness and unaffected nature. Large urns filled with colorful annuals on either side of an entry path are an even subtler delineation of entry. However, low gates and fences are less effective in creating the feeling that the garden within is a different world.

Compromising between totally barricading a property and leaving it open to view means establishing a sense of security inside, while allowing a partial view from the outside — a qualified welcome. Examples of ways to do this are decorative iron grates set in solid wooden doors, or half-hung doors set in high fences, both of which separate the inside from outside everywhere but at the entry point. If the solid fence is changed to open latticework, the

Cedars trained in a giant arch mark the entrance to a large estate.
Fruit trees lining the drive extend the drama, particularly when they are in bloom.

effect is like a veil, as compared with a heavy cloak; the treatment offers some visual inspection without physical access.

Overhead constructions contribute to a sense of entry by momentarily forcing a passage through a space of shadow after light. The deeper the arch, the greater the feeling of change as it creates enough shade to effect a decrease in temperature and a heightened sense of sanctuary from the openness on either end. An opaque structure with a full roof will likewise be felt more strongly than a light, airy structure with its more subtle effects. Height and width also affect the feeling of passage, the senses being more keenly aware of passageways hugging the body.

Natural materials such as the stone used in the patio and wall link the house to the surrounding rock garden, providing a harmonious transition. A decorative urn punctuates the departure point.

Whether standing alone or clambering up structures, plants can help define the boundary between outside and in. Archways draped in scented plants trigger our sense of anticipation for more beauty and scent beyond. A simple hedge with an opening to allow passage, or a topiary trained to form an archway, often have a softer effect than solid fences and walls, especially if the plants are light and open.

Other elements contribute to a sense of entry, as well. The entranceway is an opportunity to differentiate between the mood of the public space and the mood you want your garden to inspire, so many of the elements we looked at earlier also come into play here. The material of the walkway may change the look, feel and sound underfoot, as you go from a concrete sidewalk to a gravel path, or from lawn to flagstone. A step up or down can add to the definition of an entry point, but make sure such a change in level is easy to spot, to avoid accidents.

A metal-and-wood colonnade running in line with the patio doors draws the eye out into the garden and provides a delightful protected seating area.

The House as Entranceway

Often the main entrance to a garden is through the house. Establishing a sense of transition in this situation is just as important as creating a compelling exterior entranceway. The character of the garden will be influenced by the room that accesses it; a casual deck, for instance, would look odd coming off a formal dining room but would feel appropriate as a transition between a kitchen or family room and a garden.

Depending on how much of the garden is open to view from inside the house, it may require coordination of style and color scheme between interior and exterior, or a neutral zone to link the two if they are very different. One might step from the house onto a stone patio or wooden deck, materials that have something in common with both nature and architecture.

The height of decks and patios helps determine how quickly one feels "in" the garden. If a deck shares the same level as the elevated floor of a house, the transition will be slower, as the viewing perspective remains well above the garden. If the level of a deck or patio is closer to that of the garden, one will feel more immediately a part of the latter.

Pots of colorful annuals or raised planter boxes around the perimeter of the patio or deck further define the area as a transitional room by creating a partial barrier between it and the rest of the garden.

A pergola overhead, attached to the house, extends the ceiling line into the garden and serves to link the two while aiding the mental process of moving outdoors. Blossoming climbers can bring the scent of the garden indoors on a gentle breeze.

In cases in which the area adjacent to the house is not the best place for sitting, a covered walkway might serve as the transition, or steps with shallow risers and several landings to ease the route to the garden.

First an expanse of glass, then a broad terrace, and finally steps down a treed slope create unity between this house and its country setting.

*A grape-covered arbor dramatically links two areas in a large garden, instills a sense of journey,
and shields the eye from the vegetable patch to the side.*

Interior Walls and Gates

In a larger garden, the luxury of space allows for the creation of separate "rooms," varying in style and mood. Each transition from room to room encourages the shedding of another layer of the outer world in favor of greater involvement in the magic of the garden.

Just as with main entryways, the more absolute the barrier, the more one is likely to notice the differences on the other side. Creating barriers between spaces causes a slow-down in pace, as the visitor is prevented from taking in everything at once.

Where the desired effect is to tantalize with glimpses of what lies beyond, more open dividers, such as trellises, loose plantings, or gaps in walls, lead the viewer on. They also serve to make the space appear larger by creating a perceived middle ground.

Where a secret garden is desired, it should be exactly that, enclosed entirely by a solid leafy barricade, heavy fence or wall. The gate leading into it must be narrow enough to maintain the feeling of seclusion that is the essence of these quiet spaces.

Bright sunlight and open meadow precede a plunge into a deeply shaded cedar grove, making it feel cooler, darker and more aromatic in contrast. Transitions such as these maintain the visitor's involvement by engaging several senses at once.

Pathways

Pathways are not just a means of directing traffic through a garden. When establishing expectations, how one gets to a place is every bit as important as how one enters it. In walking along a path, clues about what is to come may stimulate our feelings of anticipation. Alternatively, paths may establish one mood to be contrasted with another at their conclusion, for an element of the unexpected.

Straight walkways encourage speed, as they represent the practical route. These are the paths of dogs and children, focused on the end point and not on the process of getting there.

Curving, crooked or meandering paths, on the other hand, slow the pace and encourage strolling and observation. An interesting sculpture or favorite specimen plant tucked into a bend in the path creates a reason to pause along the way. Massed, taller plantings or trelliswork at turns can partially hide the forward view and further direct the flow of movement. They increase the air of mystery, as they lead on without revealing fully what lies ahead.

The material chosen for a walkway also determines speed. Smooth, hard surfaces, such as flat stone, brick or interlocking pavers that are broad enough for easy navigation, move traffic more quickly. Uneven stones set in irregular patterns, unusual surfaces such as tree rounds, and intermixed materials such as pea gravel with flagstone all serve to slow traffic down.

Texture plays a part in the effect a path creates, through feel and sound. Walking on pea gravel produces a crunch and a certain distinctive give underfoot that is very tactile compared with the even hardness of flagstone or brick. Grass offers a high degree of yield and is the ultimate surface for bare feet in summer, while pine needles, shredded bark mulch or tread-

A narrow, meandering path is an invitation to take your time wandering through the plentiful flowers. Chipped stone produces a satisfying crunch underfoot and has the practical benefit of keeping feet dry regardless of weather.

*Stepping stones set in mulch
lead the way for small explorers
in a rose garden.*

able plants such as thyme provide a muffled path and delightful scent.

Not solely concerned with what is underfoot, pathways are also influenced by what is beside and overhead. Just as the degree of enclosure affects gateways, it also affects walkways through temperature changes, shadow and the muffling of sounds. Covering paths with archways or pergolas adds these dimensions — and, potentially, the scent of climbers. Walks with high sides direct the eye to the end point, where a sculpture or urn can further focus attention.

The degree of formality of the walkway is another aspect of setting expectations. Crisp, broad allées bordered on either side by neatly clipped shrubs or pollarded trees lead one to expect something formal at their end, such as a structured rose garden with traditional statuary. Their clear direction and manicured materials confirm the controlling hand of people over nature. Conversely, a meandering wood-chip path that seems to almost lose its way is an appropriate transition between cultivated garden and more natural, untamed areas.

If a site is large enough, pathways can create a sense of journey that makes each garden sojourn a fresh adventure. The feeling of exploration, surprises

Mature trees shade and cool a stone path. Their vertical mass creates a partial wall, helping to define the direction more strongly than would the path by itself.

discovered around a corner, and the delight of each separate area unfolding like a new world contain all the magic of a childhood fairy tale.

In addition to carrying more conventional topside traffic,
this bridge straddles a narrow part of a swimming pool, allowing swimmers the fun of floating beneath it

B r i d g e s

Bridges, with their tantalizing invitation to cross them, are universally compelling garden features. There is something truly enticing about the prospect of getting to the other side of a creek or stream, to explore areas that would otherwise be inaccessible to us. Who hasn't, in youth, risked a wet foot negotiating nature's stepping stones across a wilderness stream just to see what the opposite shore has to offer? More contemplative visitors may choose to pause in transit and consider the endless flow of water beneath.

A classic stone bridge is reflected in the quiet stream below. This spot encourages contemplation partway through a long journey in a walking garden of several acres.

As part of a garden walk, bridges focus one's attention completely. Whatever their scale or style, they are at their most engaging when they encourage contemplation of the act of crossing or of the mysteries in the water below. The experience of traversing even a small creek can be made more involving by creating a jog in the bridge to make the walker pause, or constructing a humpback to give the bridge the illusion of greater size. Stepping stones force one to look down and think carefully about the act of crossing the tiniest expanse of water.

On a larger scale, extended bridge walkways over bogs and ponds give the lofty sensation of being able to walk on water. Here a series of jogs may be possible to create a stroll with a most interesting ground perspective. The expansion of the humpbacked bridge into a full arch over larger rivers and ponds results in a graceful line that beautifully reflects itself in water below.

Building benches on bridges, cantilevering gazebos out over ponds, and creating islands for garden houses — these approaches make the most of water by encouraging one to take the time to sit and reflect on its surface and its depths.

The initial formality of clean, straight steps gives way to a more ragged, twisting climb. Plantings encroach increasingly as the steps progress, carrying the visitor deeper into the garden, where nature dominates and architecture recedes.

Steps and Levels

As with bridges, steps and major level changes conjure instant images. One expects the situation at the top of the steps to be different from that at the lower level. Anticipation is fueled by our understanding of other higher and lower relationships: heaven and hell, lookouts and dungeons, mountaintops and valleys. Using steps in a garden increases the sense of transition between two areas, slows the pace, contributes to the continual process of refocusing, and helps the viewer to maintain absorption in the garden.

Changes in level can create differing moods, in part because of the change in the eye's relationship to ground level. Seeing ground laid out below is like being on a hilltop, resulting in a sense of command and openness; being below the ground plane is like being in a dell, fostering a feeling of protection and enclosure.

Simple concrete steps weathered to a soft gray are further integrated into their natural surroundings by masses of climbing euonymos (Euonymous fortunei) *verging on the treads.*

The style of the steps sets the stage for what is beyond. Broad, straight and uncluttered steps are inviting because they are open and appear easy to climb. Shallow risers, broad treads and lots of landings increase their ease of use. On the other hand, narrow, meandering steps of uneven risers with plantings in their cracks are harder to negotiate, but offer an increased sense of adventure, especially if the end point cannot be seen.

These are the two ends of a spectrum between easy access and an enterprising journey; in-between are myriad compromises to delightful effect. Broad stone steps with neat plants growing along their risers have a softness that tempers their practicality. A long uphill path through woods can be made less arduous by incorporating log risers with broad treads of pea gravel or bark mulch, without compromising the journeying

Stone steps cut a subtle path up through a hillside of periwinkle and wildflowers, leading on without visually disrupting the serenity of this cool green scene.

aspect of its design. For a lengthy climb, a tantalizing glimpse of something special at the top, as you reach a bend, can provide a reason to continue the effort. A bench placed on a landing halfway offers reward for the height that's been achieved, perhaps a view, and an opportunity to prepare for the rest of the climb.

Transition devices of all kinds help visitors in their garden journey, pulling them in, taking them along, allowing them to lose themselves in the experience and feel the full power of the garden.

THE STORYTELLERS

Set beneath the light canopy of mature locust trees, paired twig chairs blend easily with the furrowed trunks. The chairs help humanize the scale of the place and are situated to catch cooling breezes and dappled shade in the heat of summer.

THE STORYTELLERS

A topiary dog trots across the lawn, animating an otherwise static scene.

Storytelling elements are the rewards of exploration, the catalysts that set the imagination loose, stir up memories and stimulate emotions. Once the essential mood has been set and the transitional elements have been passed through, these embellishments encourage flights of fancy, romantic reveries, or the peace of total contentment.

The best of these elements are personal and involving; they create communication between the garden and its owner, or its visitors. They give a garden soul. Storytellers are not just a collection of things but rather triggers for all the senses, layered over one another to form a web of experiences.

These emotional triggers play on the spirit of a place by further conjuring images in the imagination. They focus one's interest on various garden aspects, and each second of retained attention is a second more for the garden to work its magic.

A vivid blue chair contributes to the Mediterranean feel of this whitewashed concrete and stone garden.

Garden Seating

An inviting, comfortable place to sit is a prerequisite to garden contemplation. The style and nature of seating are potentially so diverse that any garden can manage to have at least one such spot, be it an elegant Lutyens-style bench in a formal setting, or a mossy, flat-topped rock in a woodland garden.

As is true for all the storyteller elements, seating best derives its style and nature from the intrinsic mood of the place. The details of the seat may instill a sense of peace through harmony with the basic garden style, or they may amuse or captivate through contrast with their surroundings.

Set on a knoll, a small gazebo beckons visitors to explore an alternate view and conjures images of romantic tête-à-têtes.

A gracefully proportioned teak bench of intricate craftsmanship could form the focal point of a formal rose garden, backed by a clipped yew hedge. When teak is simple in design and weathered to a soft gray, it subtly blends with the other natural materials of the garden in a more casual style. The same bench of pine, painted in a bright, primary color adds zing to a more modern garden in both summer and winter. For a casual country garden, a rustic covered seat made of rough-hewn branches and rampant with climbers enhances the natural beauty of the place. During a stroll in a meadow or woodland walk, a simple plank across two rocks could be all that's needed to encourage a stop along the way.

If garden seating is to be used as well as looked at, then its location in the garden requires consideration. Why should one stop and sit in this particular place? Encourage stopping in a spot that offers a variety of sensual rewards: a view or an art piece; the sound of water; cooling shade, or warm sheltered sunlight; the scent of a nearby plant.

Preferred spots for sitting change with the time of day and the seasons. A sheltered nook facing the sun may be the perfect place for enjoying the first warm days of spring or for early morning breakfasts, but the same spot may be unbearable by noon in the heat of the summer. A shady place with a reliable breeze will ensure comfort for lunch or a leisurely nap.

A plain but comfortable weathered cedar bench nestles among ferns in this cool retreat, in the company of a small stone rabbit.

Painted gray to complement the weathered barnboards at its back, a covered bench provides a rain-or-shine spot to contemplate the muted tones of the surrounding garden.

Enclosure and Shelter

The protection offered by gazebos and garden houses allows for enjoyment of the garden regardless of the weather. Sitting dry and protected while a sudden summer shower beats on the roof overhead is a sensation we enjoy from early childhood to old age. As well as the obvious practical benefits of the roof, such retreats can also provide protection from winds and, when screened, from irritating insects.

A gazebo offers visual interest even in the dead of winter.

Perched on the side of a ravine, this rustic garden house blends with the surrounding trees and feels worlds away from its location on a city lot. Views from here are spectacular in any season.

Less weatherproof, but retaining the sensation of enclosure and retreat, are bowers or covered benches. A romantic place for two to enjoy a tête-à-tête or for one to curl up with a favorite book, such cosy seating swathed in scented climbers makes its occupants feel wrapped up in the garden itself. More open still, pergolas draped in leafy vines create dappled shade beneath their canopies, with little to restrict pleasant cooling breezes from reaching those within.

Viewed from the outside, these architectural structures within the garden provide humanizing influences, hallmarks of the welcome the garden extends. The sight of them can draw one along a path, up a rise or through a forest to reach their gratifying shelter.

Textural diversity replaces the need for masses of color in this satisfying combination of tightly clipped yews,
fat-leaved hostas and the fine foliage of a cutleaf Japanese maple.
The deep color of the background wall completes a garden that is lush but elegantly restrained.

P l a n t i n g s

Generally comprising most of a garden's contents, plants and flowers are paramount contributors to its overall spirit and atmosphere. Plant selection is a topic that requires its own book — and indeed many good ones are available. For the purposes of this book, it is the mood-setting qualities of plants that we most want to consider.

As elements of bulk used to define spaces or as barriers to unwanted views, plants have a softness unmatched by artificial structures. Even tight yew hedges appear softer and more giving than wood or brick. Less formal, loose-growing shrubs give the garden three-dimensional structure in an even more relaxed manner.

When massed, plantings form powerful images through the effects of their sweep and flow, colors and shapes. Clipped topiaries, boxwood edgings and well-behaved flowers bespeak formality and grace, whereas billowing cottage plantings convey a casual, relaxed quality. Massed grasses swaying in the breeze can create a sense of movement and are reminiscent of natural prairie scenes. Densely leafed plants and tightly clipped evergreens feel heavy and shady, while delicate ones give a sense of lightness and airiness to the space.

Emerald Gaiety (Euonymous) *with its glossy, variegated foliage lends Clematis* (Jackmanii) *a boost, making the purple flowers stand out more because of the touch of white in this casual and unstudied planting.*

Individual specimens can be accents in themselves. The beauty of a mature Japanese maple, pruned carefully to reveal the graceful sweep of its branches, adds a touch of elegance. Strongly architectural perennials such as giant alliums and ornamental purple rhubarb can add drama and flamboyance to a planting scheme. Seasonal players such as the brilliant red burning bush in autumn and flowering cherries in spring will tend to dominate their area of the garden in their season of glory, but become bit players in their time off, offering only additional mass and structure.

Running wild, naturalized plantings of primrose (Primula japonica) *and buttercup* (Ranunculus repens) *find their own balance in a cheerful profusion of pink and yellow.*

Plants have the capability to change sound dramatically. Not only do they deaden external sound, they also contribute many soothing sounds in their own right, through the rustling of their leaves, and from the birds and other wildlife they attract.

Scent plays an important role in the garden, as noses have great memories. Whether the garden creates a new scent memory or stimulates an old one, the sensations can be captivating. The most commonly associated scent is, of course, the perfume of flowers and leaves, particularly compelling in the evening air. But other garden smells strike an equally deep chord: damp earth and rock after a hot rain; the fresh wood smell of cedar lattice and bark mulches; the rotting of leaves in the autumn. These scents strike chords within us, reminding us of the cycles of nature and the seasons.

The use of flowers that hold personal memories can stimulate the kind of daydreaming that helps to draw one in to the garden. You may remember fondly the sweet scent of old-fashioned lilacs in your grandmother's garden, the cheerful look of black-eyed Susans from a meadow where you used to play, or the pale pink of a particular rose that ornamented your wedding day. Indulge yourself with these reminders of happy moments past and your garden will become rewardingly personal and satisfying.

We are often not alone in our gardens. The other fauna they attract depends a great deal on what is planted. Bees love thyme, bugle blossoms and *Monarda*. Butterflies are attracted to purple, blue, yellow, and pink blossoms, while hummingbirds prefer reds and oranges, and seem to be able to find a magenta fuchsia from miles away. Berries of all kinds provide food for birds long after the height of summer has passed. Water attracts frogs and toads (who in turn help with insect control). And the shelter of dense plantings can harbor all manner of small creatures.

The sweet smell of a profusely blooming rose marks the entry to this garden with scent as well as color.

A clipped boxwood hedge bordering the steps and path carries through the mood of traditional formality set up by symmetrically placed black urns. The more exuberant daylilies and ferns planted in the borders prevent the overall effect from becoming too serious.

The power of a monochromatic scheme is demonstrated by a striking swath of purple dame's rocket (Hesperis matronalis) *growing wild at a forest's edge.*

Colour and Mood Creation

With architectural elements, focal points and flowers, color is a major factor in defining the character of a garden. Seas of harmonizing pastels or subtle neutrals are soft, restful and romantic, whereas bold masses of bright colors in equal strengths create a jolting impact and sense of excitement. A restful background scheme with a single bright accent feels lively and has a certain zing.

It is the combination of both structures and plantings that produces the overall effect. Using the simple composition of a trellis and climbing rose, consider these possible different results: in the pastel scene, a pink rose might ramble up a trellis painted classic white, soft gray or the palest of lilac; a white rose upon natural wood that has weathered to gray is subtle and neutral; for a bold look, a bright yellow rose teams with a strong mauve trellis, or deep red with blue; to create an accent, try the same red or yellow rose on an elegant background of dark green.

Color theory is a complex topic we can only touch on here, but the individual characteristics of colors and the moods they help create are important starting points. Remember that each color influences the one beside it; each combination results in a markedly different perception.

Yellow is typically happy and warm, giving a sense of space and light. It is restful in its palest hues, warmest when it tends toward sienna, and becomes a lively accent in its brighter or deeper forms. The most luminous and advancing of colors, yellows are perceived by the eye before other hues.

Greens are restful, fresh and soothing, providing the background palette and unifying force of any garden. The endless variety of this color can yield myriad

White lilies make cool blues more vivid and add a degree of luminosity to the scheme. The yellow daylily (Hemerocalis) in the foreground pops out against the receding blue lavender (Lavendula).

effects, from the sprightly pale yellow-greens of spring leaves to the calming mid-greens and cooler blue-greens, through to the rich, deep green of yew and holly. Green generally recedes and provides an equalizing force between other colors.

Blue is emotionally contradictory, being sometimes bright, intense and stimulating, and other times deep and restful, or even muted and dull. Clear blues tend to be stimulating and are elegant, rich and sophisticated in effect. Generally a cool color, blue gets warmer as it moves toward red in the spectrum. Being receding, it pushes back space, giving a sense of greater depth and size to a garden.

Pinks and mauves produce gentle and peaceful scenes in the garden, especially when mixed with grays and soft whites. While in their muted forms they are luminous in the evening, but the bright sun can wash them out to the point of being insipid unless bolstered by stronger pinks and purples in the scheme.

Flowers are not the only means of achieving color in the landscape;
boldly painted furniture and architectural elements cheer up a garden scene regardless of the season.

The hot colors of red, orange and vermilion create a bold, vibrant mood, and are effective in small quantities but somewhat tiring as a principle color scheme. Strong red is a provocative accent color, commanding and eye-catching. As red moves toward orange it becomes warmer but retains its strongly advancing quality. It is most vivid against mid-green leaves.

Neutrals in the garden help soften and unify the effects of other colors. Whites, creams, silvers, grays, taupes and browns are provided by flowers, leaves, branches and architectural structures. Used between contrasting colors, they can help marry them; used on their own, they can result in a subtle and sophisticated scene that soothes because it is undemanding.

Water

Through centuries and across nations, water has been perhaps the most cherished and highly symbolic of garden elements. It possesses countless human associations involving spiritual cleansing, baptism, rebirth, and the basis of life itself. Its fluid nature and pleasant sounds create a certain indefatigable, calming reassurance, its dark depths a sense of mysteries unfathomable. And on the hottest days of summer, even a small amount of water helps us feel refreshed.

*A still gazing-pool with waterlilies
is an ancient garden feature still popular today.*

Water features can be as simple as a filled urn with a cut blossom floating on top, or as complicated as waterfalls or Persian rills. The way in which water is used in a garden depends not just on scale and budget, but on the effect desired, the nature of the garden spirit to be drawn out.

Fast-moving water tumbling roughly over large, high rocks has a powerful, awe-inspiring effect and requires a site of suitable scale and grandeur to carry it. The intrusive sound and kinetic visual impact can provide the stunning high point in a garden possessing other strong natural or architectural features.

Quiet woodland gardens are better served by babbling streams and silent, deep pools that contribute to the mood of serenity. Their dark depths are consistent with a woodland's sense of mystery. Smooth water surfaces reflect the surrounding trees for an aura of quiet harmony rather than dramatic contrast. Soft edges planted with species that recreate a natural stream or pond habitat complete a scene that looks like it belongs to the landscape.

Waterside plantings of flag irises and grasses set up strong vertical lines,
increased in drama by their reflections in the still water and offset by the judicious placement of a large, flat rock.

One of water's most enchanting qualities is its sound when moving,
particularly useful in urban situations to counteract street noises, but soothing in any garden setting.

Formal gardens are enhanced by pools which reflect their uncluttered shapes and crisp lines. A fountain cascading water neatly into stacked reservoirs or a sculpture aiming a jet of water with studied accuracy contribute to a mood that is controlled, constructed and sophisticated.

Small urban spaces can shut out the sound of traffic and create the sound of an oasis with devices as simple and decorative as a wall fountain. These are relatively easily installed and maintained, with self-circulating water pumps and uncomplicated plumbing.

The real ruins of an old stone barn provide the perfect location for a secret garden.
A lazy drift of blue forget-me-nots leads to the rustic door, an enticement to explore the mysteries within.
Sites lacking such natural elements can achieve an equivalent end through creative follies.

Trompe l'Oeil and Follies

Where gardens lack a special natural location or are plagued by an offensive view, the imaginative craft of trompe l'oeil can often create the necessary fantasy elements out of thin air. Follies are the garden equivalent of a stage set, creating an imaginary setting and often a fictional history for a site. What could be more magical?

The centuries-old art of trompe l'oeil is most frequently executed outdoors in treillage, where the strong lines of wood can be used to trick the eye into seeing perspectives and shapes not really there. Walls turn into long tunnels, straight barriers appear to veer off at sharp angles. Clever faux finishing with paint can turn concrete into mellow blocks of rustic stone. Painters who are even more talented can turn plain walls into leafy garden extensions full of fantasy birds and animals, or miles of open hillside in the middle of the city.

Follies are picturesque buildings or walls often built to look like ruins, suggesting that the garden is ancient and enduring, with a fascinating and mysterious history. In reality, follies are new but distressed to look as though they are the product of centuries of weathering rather than a week of artistic techniques. A country property may already possess a ruined stone barn or old wall, and a garden scene can then be created around it. If not, a made-up one can look almost as realistic. City gardens may likewise benefit from protrusions of old stone walls or a deep and secluded recess.

Mirrors can also be used to trick the eye, adding space and dimension. Just as in interior use, their placement requires careful consideration of just what will be reflected from all possible viewing angles, with the added consideration of sun reflection. Set in walls or hedges, they can visually transform archways into whole new gardens that do not really exist.

A mirror makes this tiny side garden appear much more expansive, reflecting the Japanese maple and pond in front of it.

A traditional cherub holding birds represents spring, one of a set of four seasonal icons, each placed at a corner of this square garden.

Statuary and Objets Trouvés

Statuary in a garden can turn a setting from an empty stage into a tableau of momentarily frozen action. Such a scene provides the necessary jumping-off point for a flight of fancy. When the imagination takes over, lifelike statues of animals, cherubs and mythical creatures satisfy our longings to make our gardens places where nature is at home and the fairies really do come out to play.

Abstract statuary provides a source of contemplation, reminiscent of watching clouds go by as you lie on your back in the summer grass. They can be many things and make many statements, depending

Driftwood in the shape of a chicken has been wittily set upon a nest of smooth stones.

Some of the most endearing garden elements are personal rather than grand. This camouflaged frog is a reward for the perceptive viewer.

on the viewer. This kind of interaction between the visitor and objects in the garden helps to personalize the experience, making the garden more memorable.

Traditional statues can be representational, such as the popular theme of the four seasons rendered in stone figures. They may remind us of other times and places, tell a little story of their own, or add a whimsical touch to the garden. Sometimes the way a statue came to you is important in itself. If it was handed down through the family, or obtained on a special trip abroad, then every time you look at it, you will be reminded of people and places past.

A selection of modern art pieces sits in stark contrast to the sweep of green pasture in the background.
The sculptural form of ornamental onion blossoms in the foreground mirrors the abstract shapes.

Such effects are not dependent on store-bought works of art. Many found objects can be enchanting by virtue of unusual form, texture and placement within the garden. Rocks offer diverse possibilities if one looks for the unique: massive granite boulders with subtle color variations for gardens of suitable scale; perfectly round, smooth stones set amongst flowers in textural and geometric juxtaposition to the softer foliage; Druidic arrangements of stone on stone as a type of freeform sculpture in a modern garden.

Similarly, branches, stumps and driftwood, in evocative shapes, can create imaginative features for natural settings.

Placement plays an important role in the effect of art in the garden. At the end of a vista, art draws one along. At a bend in the path, tucked around foliage or half-hidden under shrubbery, it provides a sense of discovery. A sculpture can soften an expanse of hedge or wall, give a reason to stop or sit, or add a sense of scale and instantly humanize a space.

SUMMARY

These, then, are some of the means to creating a garden that truly speaks to you and to others who visit it. First, recognize and foster the inherent spirit that is your garden's initial promise. Marry it to your own vision of special places, to provide the transitional elements that help render one receptive to the garden and all that lies within it. Transitions are the keys that unlock the doors to that part of ourselves that feels with all the senses and responds more from the heart than from the head. Finally, inject into the scene those things that will make the garden yours; things that tell of where you've been, who you've known, and what you love.

In this way, for you and for those with whom you share it, your garden becomes a personal paradise of captured memories and future possibilities, a haven that lets you dream your dreams, whatever they may be, far removed from the bustle of an everyday world.

Demonstrating the power that can be derived from the imaginative juxtaposition of even simple elements, this artful composition combining smooth and rough, hard and soft, stark and lush invites the viewer to pause and contemplate its yin-yang quality.